GET MORE DONE

*How To Get More Done By 0900
Than Most People Do All Day*

Dr. Malcolm Upton

Get More Done: How To Get More Done By 0900 Than Most People Do All Day
Copyright © 2018 by Malcolm Upton. All Rights Reserved.

All rights reserved. No part of this book may be reproduced in any form or by any electronic or mechanical means including information storage and retrieval systems, without permission in writing from the author. The only exception is by a reviewer, who may quote short excerpts in a review.

Malcolm Upton

Printed in the United States of America

Second Edition: Nov 2018
North Texas Mastermind Community

CONTENTS

What's Important? What's Urgent? What's The Difference? 1
How Can I Accomplish More By Doing Less? 5
How Can I Schedule Success? 9
Stones, Pebbles, Sand, and Water 11
How Do You Make Your Goals SMARTER? 13
The $1,500,000 Frog 21
Experience or Wisdom? 23
Choose Wisely 29

WHAT'S IMPORTANT? WHAT'S URGENT? WHAT'S THE DIFFERENCE?

GETTING MORE DONE...
That may seem like an elusive goal to you right now, but, like many goals in life, the main two things standing between you and your goal are the skills to do it and the will to succeed.

If you didn't have at least some will to succeed, you would still be stuck below the line (more on that later) complaining that life isn't fair, waiting for the lightning bolt of success to strike, and quietly desperate when it doesn't.

But you are reading this instead...

You have at least the seeds of the will to succeed (who knows, you might have a whole forest of will to succeed) - and seeds are all you need to start with.

Now, let's get you some skills. If you take the skills, use the seeds of the will to put them in place, you will start to see success. The more success you see, the more those seeds of the will to succeed will grow. The more they grow, the more you will use the skills - it becomes a virtuous cycle spiraling you to ever higher heights.

What skill should we start with then? How about your own success schedule, built just for you and your success?

Get whatever you use to keep your schedule now. Outlook, a kitten calendar, an expensive day planning book - whatever you have the most comfort and skill with. You can use it for all the things you are currently doing with it, but you are going to start scheduling some additional appointments - with yourself - to help you do the important things in life.

Note, I said the important things in life, you probably already have the urgent things scheduled. So what's the difference?

Important things have large values for you. It might be a big value to a relationship you have, or a big potential return for the value of your business, or whatever. The point is that there is a lot of value - to you - to spending that time in that activity. Urgent things have a deadline - a time they are expected to be done by - usually expected by someone else.

You may be asking, "Aren't they the same thing?" It is true that most people see urgent and important as the same, and sometimes they are, but not always.

For example - attending your son's graduation ceremony - important, urgent, or both?

It's important to him because he only graduates once. Since it is so important to him and he is important to you, it would be important to you too. It only happens at that specific time on that specific day so it would be also be urgent.

Let's try another one. Paying taxes - important, urgent, both, or neither?

Let's break it down. If you don't do it on time it costs you even more money, so that would make it urgent. On the other hand, it really doesn't do much for you, at least not directly, so it wouldn't be very important. Paying taxes is one of those examples of something that isn't important, but that we can't ignore.

What about spending time with your spouse or significant other.

Fact is that may be one of the reasons you're reading this - because your bride is getting mighty tired of feeling like she is playing second fiddle to your work or business. But there isn't a deadline on spending time with your spouse. That's one of the reasons it's so hard to make time for her/him. It's a classic example of something that is important but not urgent.

We have Urgent & Important, Urgent, and Important. What would be an example of something that is neither important nor urgent?

I'm not sure - maybe playing games on your phone or some such. Don't get me wrong - nothing against a little down time - and they can serve a very useful function in allowing us to take a mental "walk around the block" when we are waiting in line or something. But that doesn't make it or dozens of other things either urgent or important.

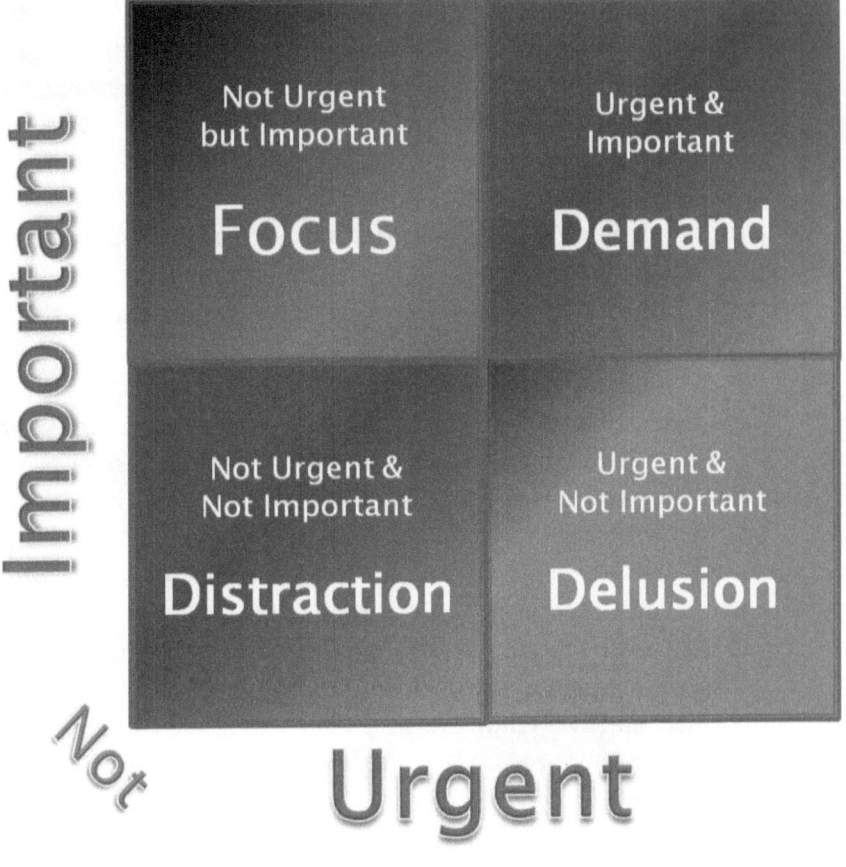

Figure 1 - Important/Urgent quadrants

So you can put all your activities in one of four areas. The lower left quadrant is those things that are neither important nor urgent – playing games. These are the seas of distraction where, if we aren't careful, we can pour our time out and get nothing in return. Most mature people recognize the danger of spending too much time here. Those who don't tend to be in trouble a lot with bosses, significant others, and anyone else that depends on them – because they go for a swim in the distraction sea – and don't get something urgent done...

Next is the lower right quadrant of things that are urgent, but not important - paying taxes. Too often we are deluded into thinking that just because someone else thinks it is important, that it is important to us - but that is not necessarily true. This is part of the trap of most jobs. Those who are trapped in a job often spend all their time at work doing things that are urgent for others, but not important to them – and then spend their time away from work mostly swimming in the distraction sea. They rarely, if ever, invest any time in what is truly important – and then only in things from the Demand quadrant above it.

Next is the upper right quadrant of things that are both important and urgent - attending graduation or another significant event. These are important things that demand our attention - and we ignore them at our peril.

But the upper left quadrant – important and not urgent – is the realm of true leverage for improving yourself, your business, any area of your life. The realm of Focused activity. It is the realm that successful people have learned to harness in order to take control of where their life is going.

Focused activities are important but not urgent. Focused activity is where we sharpen the ax so we can cut more efficiently. Focused activities are where an investment of a little time results in more effective marketing, more efficient processes, a more valuable business. Focused activities are where we replace the ax with a chainsaw. Focused activities will not happen if we allow everyone else - with their urgent claims - to dictate our schedule. Focused activities are what we make time for in our Success Schedule.

HOW CAN I ACCOMPLISH MORE BY DOING LESS?

IT SEEMS TO MAKE PRACTICAL SENSE - the more results you want, the more projects you should get started working on. Problem is - it doesn't work out that way.

Research has proven this over and over, but just drawing a simple picture will show you why this is the case...

Let's say you've identified four projects you can work on over the next little while and, if you get these four projects done, each one of them will provide a massive boost to your profits. Each project will take about a month's worth of Focus Times and such to get done. Common wisdom is for you to start working on all four at once to start reaping the rewards.

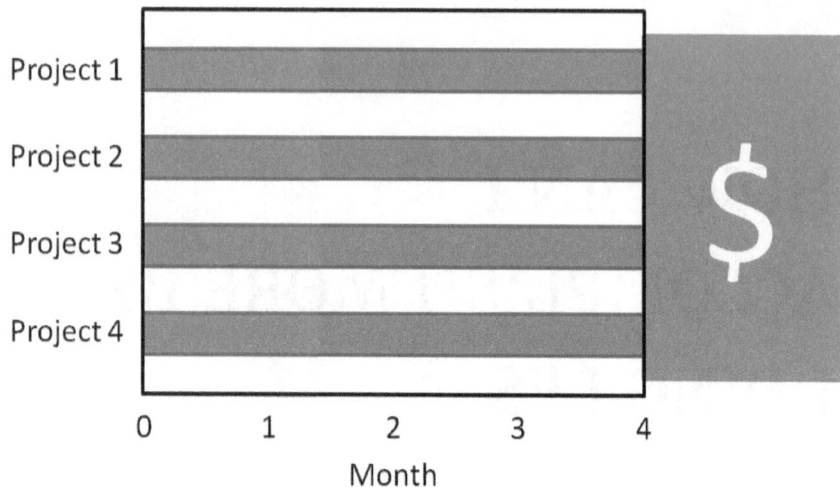

Figure 2 - Start All Projects At Once

This is an example of how confusing the map for the terrain can get us in trouble.

We talk about "planting seeds" and "nurturing a project" and "harvesting the benefits" like we are growing plants on a farm - but the fact is that many of the things a crop of vegetables need, don't have anything to do with projects. In this case, plants have a growing season. If you want 4 fields of our cash crop (cotton was big in my home town) you have to plant all 4 fields at the same time, wait for the end of the growing season, and harvest them at the same time.

But projects don't have a growing season...

What if, instead, you started Project 1, and only Project 1, and got that puppy done. And then, as you started harvesting the benefits of Project 1, you start Project 2, and only Project 2, until it is done. And so on. You would still get Project 4 done at the same time, and you would still get all the benefits you would have received if you had started all the projects at once. But Project 3 will give you an additional month of benefits. Project 2 will give you an additional two months of benefits. Project 1 will give you an additional three months of benefits. Do you want more - or less?

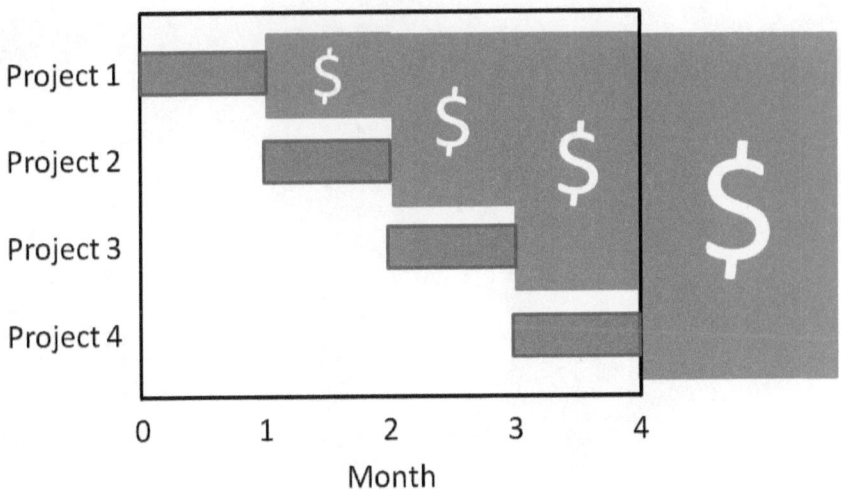

Figure 3 - One Project At A Time

Dr. Malcolm Upton

HOW CAN I SCHEDULE SUCCESS?

THE SINGLE MOST IMPORTANT THING IN THIS WHOLE BOOK is this. If you don't get anything else out of this book - get this. The single most important "big rock" you need to be sure is in your schedule every single week is Focus Time. Every single week, once a week (at least) for an hour and a half to two hours, shut the office door, turn off the phone, ignore the email and social media alerts, and focus on one project that is important, but not urgent. It might be a new marketing campaign, updating your sales script, putting together a new standard operations procedure, determining what your Critical Community Contribution is - something that will have lasting value, but doesn't have an external deadline.

Your Success Schedule will have three general types of activities on it. "Work in" time, "Work on" time, and "Work for" time. This is the "Work on" time, called Focus Time. It is one (maybe two) blocks of time every week that you set aside to spend 1.5-2 uninterrupted hours specifically working on a project that will help your business grow. For example: New marketing materials, plans for a new marketing campaign, developing a new product/service, something that builds your business up.

It is also important that you focus on one thing. Remember the previous chapter. Try to finish the project in a single focus time. If you can't, use the next focus time for that specific project again. Get one done before moving on to another.

Focus time
Every week
Your Success Schedule also has "Work for" time - time that is devoted outside your business to those things that you work for. This can be subdivided, but husbands - make sure you put Date Night on the schedule every week. In fact, it is the only thing that should go on the schedule

before Focus Time. Just like Focus Time, Date Night can be moved – but should *never be cancelled*.

The heart of the Success Schedule is identifying the Important, non-Urgent activities - the big rock activities - in our life and make time for them first. What are big rock activities? Let me tell you a story in the next chapter.

STONES, PEBBLES, SAND, AND WATER

THE STORY IS TOLD of a Time Management Master who was approached by his young apprentice.

"Tell me, master, how can I get important things done when I am so busy with everything else?"

The Master smacked Grasshopper on the head shouting, "You are never busy!"

Grasshopper uncrossed his eyes, bowed, and said, "Apologies, Master, I forgot that busy is an illusion – it is all priorities. How can I change my priorities to get more important things done?"

"Ah, Grasshopper, go and get a jug, five large stones, a sack of pebbles, a sack of sand, and a pitcher of water."

Puzzled, Grasshopper went and retrieved the items.

"Now, Grasshopper, place the stones in the jug"

Grasshopper did as he was asked...

"Now, place as many pebbles as you can in the jug"

Grasshopper did as he was asked...

"Now, place as much sand as you can in the jug"

Grasshopper did as he was asked...

"Now, fill the jug with as much water as it will hold"

Grasshopper did as he was asked...

"Grasshopper, the jug is your time, the items you put into it your activities. What is the lesson of the jug?"

Grasshopper thought for a moment, "Master, the lesson is that no matter what is on your schedule, you can always fit something else in?"

"No!" the Master shouted, smacking him on the head, "The lesson, O thick one, is this - how many stones would have fit if you had started with the water?"

First lesson is that busy is an illusion – an excuse. We all have the same numbers of hours in the day. People who are "busy" use that as an excuse for poor prioritization.

Second lesson is that demands and delusions (pebbles and sand) are going to tend to get done unless we specifically say "no" to them. Actually, this is a skill I have coached more than one person on. If you are one of those people that always says "yes" to anyone's urgent activity, whether it is important or not, here is a tool you can use to get more control in your life. Get a 3x3 sticky note in a bright color (neon pink or yellow work well). Get a marker that will contrast well with the color of the sticky note (black is fine). In the largest letters that will fit on the sticky note, clearly print the word "NO" and put the sticky note where you will see it when people are burying you in "should". Use this word as needed to get out from under the "should" pile...

Distractions (water) also tend to show up a lot. Because of our default human mindset distractions will, like water, tend to flow in to fill all the available space in your schedule that isn't allocated somewhere else.

The key to scheduling success is to start scheduling the important, focus activities - the large stones - so that you actually start getting their benefits on a consistent basis.

HOW DO YOU MAKE YOUR GOALS SMARTER?

MANY OF YOU HAVE HEARD one of the several interpretations of SMART goals – and the SMARTER acronym we use in the Focused Business Community are definitely based on those SMART acronyms. But since I have a doctorate – and the license to build models – I decided to improve on the SMART acronym and make it more powerful.

Here's what it looks like...

S	Specific: here you want to be sure you put down, specifically, what you want to accomplish. The idea is to word the goal in a way that it lies completely within your control to complete or not and that you know specifically what actions to take (or at least the first specific actions to take). So, for example, instead of "get more leads from a marketing system", which lies at least partially outside your control (get more leads) and is vague (a marketing system) – making it specific by saying, "Implement the authority engine marketing system". This is a very specific marketing system with very specific pieces that would need to be put into place and it lies entirely within your span of control.

M

Measurable: Again, most of the acronyms have "Measurable" as the "M" – because if you can't measure it, you don't really know if you've completed it. Measurable may be a business result that improves like, "Get an average of 10 leads a week." It may also be an activity measurement, "Run the system for at least 4 weekly cycles before the end of the quarter." It may be a deliverable completed, "Complete 4 Authority Engine weekly packages – ready to post" or a specific task accomplished, "Set up active accounts on YouTube, SoundCloud, LinkedIn, Medium, and FaceBook." The whole idea is to have an objective, unambiguous method of telling that the goal has been accomplished.

A

Aligned: The next letter in the acronym is one of those that has a lot of variations. For the purposes of us in the Focused Business Community, "A" stands for **Aligned** – Too often, especially in large organizations, goals are not aligned, or at least no obvious, explicit alignment, to the purpose of the organization. This is a reminder to make the alignment explicit. Ideally, the goal aligns directly and explicitly to the Vision, Mission, and/or Values of the organization. Sometimes, it is enough for you to align it to Strategic, or other goals that do have that direct, explicit alignment.

Goals that are clearly tied to your Vision, Mission, Values, Strategic Goals, and/or higher order goals are more engaging, more inspiring and more likely to be accomplished than goals that either aren't tied to one of those overarching items, or goals where the tie is not clearly made. One nice thing about building goals at the Strategy Implementation Summits is that you have this tie very clearly made, since every sticky you put together was made in response to a review of that business area in light of where you stand on your Strategic (1 year) goals.

R

Realistic: The next letter, the first "R" can be a little harder to get right, but it is important to do your best to make your goals Realistic – The challenge here is that you will get the most out of having goals that are a stretch of your current abilities. Why is that? I'd like you to do a quick exercise with me. I want you to put your arms straight up above your head. Put them up as far as you can. If you are able to, stand up and put them over your head – you can reach higher that way. Make sure they are as high over your head as you can get them. Now for the "a-ha" moment...

Stretch your hands just a little bit higher...

You can put your arms down now. Almost everyone is able to stretch just a little bit higher – despite the fact that we thought we were already at full extension. Your non-conscious mind tends to keep back just a little bit of capability all the time. This is one reason that physical therapy with a trained physical therapist is so valuable – they help us stretch just a little bit higher. Your goals can be the same way – if you set realistic goals, then stretch them just a bit, you will find out that you often can reach just a little bit higher. On the other hand, if you consistently set goals that are unrealistically high, and continually fail to achieve them, your non-conscious mind, in order to protect you from the pain of failure, will start to shy away from the entire goal setting activity.

Two things you can do to improve the realism of your goals and tap into the power of stretching while minimizing the negative consequences of missing goals that are set too high is to make every goal two tiered. There is the goal that you are sure you can reach – "Run the Authority Engine marketing system 3 successive weeks" and also a stretch goal – "Stretch Goal: run the system for the 6 successive weeks prior to next Strategy

Summit." The second thing you can do is a review of your goal setting for the previous quarter – how did you do? If you consistently set your goals too high, make sure to back off a little this quarter. If you met all of your stretch goals last quarter – maybe you should set those as tier 1 goals with higher stretch goals this quarter.

This is a reminder to be sure that something is possible. This is <u>not</u> intended to discourage stretch goals or big, hairy, audacious goals (BHAGs). If the goal is to increase sales to 1,000 next month, and last month was 750 - that is a BHAG, but potentially reachable. If the goals is to increase sales to 1,000 and last month was 75 - maybe a reassessment is in order.

T

Time bounded: The "T" in our acronym is the same as most others. Basically this is setting boundaries in time.

When will you start, if you join us for the Strategy Implementation Summit, this is accomplished when you move your sticky to the calendar.

When will you be finished? – This is when the specific (remember the 'S') outcomes will be measurable (remember the 'M').

Depending on how complex the goal is, you might want to put more than just a start and end time. If you are going to have major phases to the project, then do the same thing we did for your strategic goals. For them, we have a final goal based on the answers to the four strategic planning questions, but we also have intermediate goals at the 1, 3, and possibly 5 year points between now and then. If you have a complex project with intermediate deliverables, you do the same thing, but instead of deciding where you will be toward the final goal at the various time milestones, you figure out when you will have completed the goal milestones.

E

Emotionally Engaged: One of the fundamental guiding principles empowering the Focused Business Community understanding of the way life really works is that humans are, at their heart, emotional creatures. We are motivated by our emotions. I mean, just look at how I just explained all of that – rational thought and logic played no part of the description.

You get better results when you are engaged and inspired – but engagement and inspiration are both emotional states. If all you do is make your goals SMART – where is the emotional engagement? Where is the emotional inspiration?

The 'E' is all about taking a moment when you are building your goals to consciously identify the emotionally engaging aspects of your goal so that you are more likely to remain engaged and inspired and, ultimately, successful in achieving the goal. Elsewhere we talk about the fact that benefits are emotionally-charged results we get from something.

What are the benefits for you of achieving this goal? How will "complete" look/feel/sound? Tapping into the emotions that will come with accomplishment – visualizing the look/feel/sound of completion – will help you stay engaged and inspired to act on your goals with open eyes to make them possible...

One of the things that helps Nancy (our Non-Conscious mind) reset the filters to enable success is if we get emotionally engaged with a goal. This is why visualization always has a sensory and/or emotional component to it. What is in it for you? How will "complete" look/feel/sound to you?

R Resourced: Around the turn of the century, when I was practicing as a process improvement coach, one of the popular things we dealt with was the Employee Empowerment craze. Managers would read or hear about a company that was empowering its employees and getting incredible results in productivity, engagement, and creativity – and they wanted some of that. Unfortunately, most of the time the way they would go about it is they would do what many unskilled mangers do when they try to delegate. Instead of empowering the employees (or even just delegating to them) they would abdicate responsibility and leave the employees to flounder in waters way over their head – then punish them when they failed.

What we would teach them to do instead, and what I teach my community members when they start delegating, was to make sure everything was in place before empowering (or delegating). This is why we have the Resourced 'R' in SMARTER goals. It is to remind you to take a bit of time when fleshing out the goal to figure out what you will need to accomplish this goal. What skills, materials, prior completed projects, community support, coaching support, money, other resources, and, especially, time will you need. Of all of these, time to focus on completing the goal is perhaps the most important. In fact, the only requirement for this portion of a SMARTER planning form is to designate which Focus Time or Times from your Success Schedule you will dedicate to completing this goal.

At the Strategy Implementation Summit, we take each of the goal stickys we moved to the calendar and fill out a SMARTER planning form on them. That way we are as fully empowered as possible to achieve the goals for the coming quarter that will keep us on track to getting to "Someday I'll…"

	One of the pitfalls many "Empowerment" efforts in the last part of last century fell into was giving people authority (and responsibility) for something, but failing to give them the resources to be successful. This second R reminds you to identify the resources: skills, materials, prior completed goals, people's time (and which people), community support, coaching support, etc..

Dr. Malcolm Upton

THE $1,500,000 FROG

WHEN ANDREW CARNEGIE WAS TOLD the secret in this section, he wrote the person who told him a check that, in today's dollars, was worth at least $1,500,000. Maybe it would be worth a few words here...

There is a guy who is a legend in our community for three reasons. First, he's probably the happiest guy around, always optimistic and seeing the good in any situation. Second, he is the most dependable person you could ever know, especially when it comes to tasks that are hard, gross, or otherwise something the rest of us try to put off or avoid all together. Third, however, is his breakfast...

You see, Uncle Joe eats the most unique breakfast I can imagine. Every day, he gets up, goes out to the marsh behind his house, catches a frog, and eats it raw. One time I asked him why he ate such a disgusting breakfast and Uncle Joe replied, "Well, ya see it's this way, after I eat my frog first thing, I figger nothing worse can happen for the rest of the day..."

I tell you that story not to encourage you to start eating live frogs for breakfast, but to make a different point. We all have tasks that seem to be as unwelcome as eating a frog. Tasks we put off, avoid, and, too often, don't get done when we should. Curiously enough, they also tend to be tasks that we need to do to work on our business instead of just in it.

Part of the discipline of planning is setting priorities, scheduling tasks, and otherwise trying to maximize the time you spend on important tasks - some of which are frogs to eat. One way I do this, and the secret that Andrew Carnegie paid $1,500,000 for, is this.

Last thing every work day, you should sit down and plan for the next work day. When you do, choose four important tasks to get done, no more. Write them down on a whiteboard or somewhere you will see them easily all day long. Make sure one of them is a frog you have to eat (unless they are all taken care of - something that may occur on rare occasions). Put the frog you have to eat at the top of the list and, if at all possible, do it first thing the next work day morning, before tackling the other three important tasks.

This way you get the advantage of Uncle Joe's breakfast, you get an important task you don't want to do out of the way, and can concentrate on a manageable list of important tasks you are more willing to do for the rest of the day. If you don't eat your frog first, it is likely that you will find yourself doing unimportant tasks and rationalizing instead of eating the frog.

Eat your frog each day – the day will be more productive when you do...

EXPERIENCE OR WISDOM?

THE OTHER DAY, we were sitting around the table in the coffee shop trying to help Bubba get himself out of a fix he was in. We were also trying to keep from laughing at him because it was such a greenhorn mistake. Now, all of that wouldn't be too bad, but Bubba has been working in his business for 20 years and should have graduated to a whole new level of mistakes. Unfortunately, Bubba is a (fictional) example of someone we probably all know, someone we may occasionally see when we look in the mirror. Bubba is an example of someone who doesn't have the wisdom of 20 years of experience, because they've had one year of experience 20 times...

The other day, we were sitting around the table in the coffee shop trying to help Bubba get himself out of a fix he was in. We were also trying to keep from laughing at him because it was such a greenhorn mistake. Now, all of that wouldn't be too bad, but Bubba has been working in his business for 20 years and should have graduated to a whole new level of mistakes. Unfortunately, Bubba is a (fictional) example of someone we probably all know, someone we may occasionally see when we look in the mirror. Bubba is an example of someone who doesn't have the wisdom of 20 years of experience, because they've had one year of experience 20 times...

Experience is what happens when you try something new: a new pricing structure, a new advertising campaign, or a new marketing channel. Sometimes the experience is positive - the pricing structure better reflects the quality of your service and you not only improve your margins, but you increase your sales as well. Sometimes the experience is so-so, your new advertising campaign hits the breakeven point, but only gets a little above that. Sometimes the experience is like Bubba's, a negative one, you try a new marketing channel and get no leads from it.

Experience happens every time you try something. It happens to anyone who is at all active, all the time. Wisdom, however, is what you can accumulate to take you to those higher levels, the levels that Bubba has yet to reach despite all his time in his business.

How do you turn experience into wisdom? By closing the learning cycle. If you do an Internet search on "Learning cycle" you'll get a million hits (just like anything) and most of them were invented by Doctors with PhD's and MEd's and such after their name. A lot of papers and dissertations have been written on them to advance academic careers and I wish them all the joy of their accomplishments. But one thing I learned from my stay in the Ivory Tower - just because a doctor of something invented it, doesn't mean it's right, and even if it is right, they tend to be under pressures that make it hard for them to make something useful to those of us out in the field where we get mud on our boots and dirt in our eyes.

Something else those years gave me, however, was my own Doctor of Management - so now I have a license to make up my own models (or customizations of models) and since I'm not trying to advance my academic career, I can make it as useful as I want...

So what does a closed learning cycle, a wisdom generating cycle, look like? Well, maybe it would be best to start with what Bubba's non-wisdom generating experiences look like.

Before we do anything, we think about it first - even if it is just getting

Think

an idea and not thinking it through (like the famous "Red Neck's Last Words" - "Hey, Vern, watch this..."). So whether it is a budding Solomon, or just Bubba, the first step is going to be to think of something to do.

After we think of what we're going do, including the planning (however shallow that is), the next obvious thing is that we do something.

Think   Do

That is blindingly obvious and a lot of people who are Outstanding In Their Field of academics would like to yank my Doctorate card for daring to call this a model, but remember, I'm trying to talk to people out standing in their field of life, and I think blinding flashes of the obvious are good things. But to throw the academics a bone, maybe we should at least put an arrow in it...

Think   Do

So this is Bubba's experience engine, Think->Do, Think->Do, Think->Do, year after year, the same "lessons" over and over with little or no learning taking place, little or no wisdom being accumulated. Bubba is like a battery-operated robot at the bottom of a staircase - walk into the stairs, bounce back, walk into the stairs, bounce back, over and over again. How do we break out of that mindless repetition? You do the same thing that Architects, Doctors, and many other professionals do in their practice, you close the learning cycle with a Review.

One of the things practicing professionals do on a regular basis, one of the reasons they call it a practice, is that they review their actions to see what they can learn from them. Doctors review cases - their own and others, sometimes alone, often in a group, to see what they did well, what they could have done better, and what they can do in general to improve their ability to practice medicine in the future. In the Air Force, we would have a "Hot Wash" after each major exercise or event and everyone - including the commander (if s/he was a good one) would be honest about what went well and what each individual could do, in their own sphere of action, to make a similar activity go better next time. You can do the same thing - and get the same valuable results.

When you are thinking about doing something new, plan - at least a little - and include time afterward to review what you can learn from the action. After you've completed the advertising campaign, sale, hired the new person, or whatever, sit down with everyone concerned and have a hot wash review. This can be especially valuable if you have someone (like a coach) who wasn't part of the action sit in and help keep the discussion above the line (personal ownership, accountability, and responsibility) instead of it dropping into a finger-pointing session that is a waste of everyone's time.

Walk through the action - what went well, what should we do better next time, what should we not do that we did this time, what should we do next time that we didn't do this time? Keep everyone focused on "I did/didn't..." and "Next time I can..." Then capture what you've learned in scripts, procedures, or at least notes for the next time you try that.

By adding a review to close the learning cycle loop every time, you will cycle up the stairs, one stair at a time, gaining wisdom with every experience. It won't stop you from making mistakes, but it will close the door on one level of mistakes, lock in the value you can get there, and open up your vistas to a whole new universe of mistakes - no, not mistakes, opportunities to learn.

Here's to your wisdom generating success and wisdom generating opportunities to learn. Who knows, maybe we'll call you Solomon one of these days...

Dr. Malcolm Upton

CHOOSE WISELY

NEAR THE END OF THE MOVIE *Indiana Jones and the Last Crusade*, those who have reached the chamber where the Holy Grail resides are counseled to "Choose wisely." The Nazi's who don't end up dying gruesomely. When Indy does – he is able to save his father's life.

One of the most powerful secrets any of us can learn is to choose wisely. Let me explain...

The Line

We were sitting in the coffee shop again and Bubba was really on a tear. He was blaming the government for the economy, and using the economy as an excuse for why his business wasn't doing well. Although denial is not a river in Egypt so much blame, excuses, and denial, were flowing from Bubba that you would think he was the Nile.

So, here was Bubba going on and on, and finally I said, "Eeep."

But Bubba just kept on going.

So I tried again and said, "Eeep."

This time, Bubba, looked at me, but he kept on going.

So I tried one more time, "Eeep."

Bubba stopped, looked at me funny, and said, "Why are you 'Eeepin'?"

I looked at him and said, "Bubba, that's a word trying to get in edgewise."

After everyone had quit laughing, I explained.

"When we blame other people, or make excuses about how we can't do it, or even deny that there is a problem or at least deny that we have anything to do with it, how much power do we have in the situation?"

Everyone thought on that for a while and allowed that they wouldn't have much power in that case.

"Well," I said, "blame, excuses, and denial are an acronym."

"Not another acronym," muttered Joe.

"Yes, Joe," I said, "another acronym. Blame, excuses, and denial, are B - E - D. What does that spell?"

Mutters of "bed" came from around the table.

"That's right," I said, "and how much progress can you make when you are stuck in BED?"

They all allowed that you couldn't make much progress stuck in BED.

"The same is true about blame, excuses, and denial. If we stay stuck there, blaming others, making excuses, and denying that we have anything to do with it, what do we sound like?"

They all thought about that for a minute and then Joe said, "Sounds like a victim to me."

"Exactly, Joe, blame, excuses, and denial are the victim's mindset. In fact, when we are in that mindset, the part of our brain that is responsible for coming up with new ideas goes dark – we literally can't think of anything to do.

"On the other hand, what if we took ownership of at least some of the situation? What if we became accountable for what we could control? What if we took responsibility instead? What kind of power would we have then?"

They all thought on that for a while and allowed that they would have a lot more power in that case.

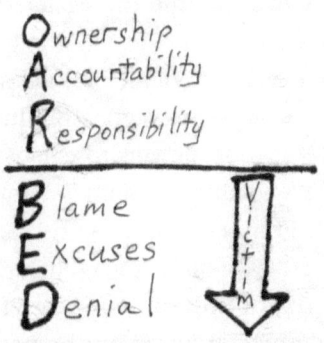

"You see, ownership, accountability, and responsibility, are another acronym. O - A - R, what is that?" I asked.

"It's an oar - like in a boat," said Sally.

"That's right," I replied, "and if we get hold of that oar we will always be able to make progress, even if it's slow."

"And what kind of mindset does ownership, accountability, and responsibility sound like?"

Again, Sally had the answer, "Sounds like a victor to me."

"That's right, Sally. Not surprising, when people focus on what they can take ownership, accountability and responsibility for – that part of their brain where we come up with creative ideas lights back up again. It turns back on our ability to come up with solutions.

"So and which one would you rather be, a victim, or a victor? Would you rather be powerless and stuck in BED, or have at least some power by taking hold of your OAR?"

We call this being above or below the line. Below the line is the realm of the victim, where we are stuck in BED. Above the line is the realm of the victor, where we use our hold on our OAR to make progress in our situation. Most people in most situations will naturally fall below the line. However, we always have a choice: we can choose to stay below the line, or we can choose to live above the line instead. The more often we choose to be above the line, the more power we will have in our situation. It is also true that the more often we choose to be above the line the easier it is to make that choice.

I first really became aware of this when I read Dr. Victor Frankel's book *Man's Search For Meaning*. In that book he says, "Between stimulus and response there is a space. In that space is our power to choose our response. In our response lies our growth and our freedom." If anyone knows of what they speak, it would be Dr. Frankel – because he came to this realization while strapped to an experimental table in a Nazi concentration camp. He had more excuses than I hope any of us ever have – but he didn't focus on those – he focused on what he retained ownership of – his mind. As he suffered through that horrible experience he chose to consider, "How will I explain this to my students..." because he was, and would be again, a professor at the University of Vienna.

We Fall Down, We Get Up

Bubba flopped into his chair at the coffee shop and let out a huge sigh, "Coach, I'm just plum tuckered out. Seems like everything has gone wrong this past week and it is just wiping me out..."

"I'm sorry to hear that, Bubba. What have you learned from your trials?"

"Don't you want to hear what's happened first?"

"If you need to tell me, that's OK, but focusing on what went wrong beyond what you can learn from it really isn't very helpful."

Bubba looked a little confused. "But the rest of us always talk about what went wrong. We're still talking about some of the bone-headed things Vern and I did in High School."

I had to shake my head because I'd heard some of those stories. Sometimes I'm amazed Bubba and Vern survived – and stayed out of jail...

"Bubba, Ralph Waldo Emerson said, 'Finish each day and be done with it. You have done what you could; forget them as soon as you can. Tomorrow is a new day; you shall begin it serenely and with too high spirit to be encumbered with your old nonsense.' Now, Ralph was a smart guy, but he was also an academic at a time when $20 words were a lot more common. Applying Dr. Malcolm's KISS (Keep It Super Simple) to that –

what he was saying is don't focus on what happened - focus on now and the near future. If you hold on to what went wrong - your old nonsense - it will just hold you back from what you can achieve."

"I guess I can kinda' see that, Coach."

"Remember the song by Bob Carlisle where the guy in the village thought the monks must have a perfect life. Then he asked a monk what it was like and the monk said 'We fall down, we get up'. Barbara Cocoran from Shark Tank said in an interview with Success magazine that the most important quality she looks for in a potential business partner is the willingness to get back up again."

"No kidding?"

"No kidding, Bubba. In Bob Carlisle's song, the guy is real disappointed at first in the monk's answer - but his attitude changes when he thinks about it some. What do you think about your tough week now?"

Bubba thought for a minute, "I'm thinking we should figure out what I can learn from it, put that stuff back into my processes and such, and then I should just forget it and drive on."

"Sounds like a good plan to me, Bubba..."

Punjis, Potholes, or Portals

So mistakes. How many of you made a mistake in the last two hours?

Fact is. Mistakes happen. As long as you're trying (and as a business owner, you better be trying) you're going to make mistakes.

If we are going to stay above the line and not just deny we made a mistake, there's three general ways to approach the mistakes. There's a common way to deal with mistakes. There's a better way to deal with them, and there's a genius way to deal with them.

So, commonly, if people don't deny the mistake entirely, we treat mistakes like punji sticks.

You may remember Vietnam, others of you have studied it. But one of the big differences between Vietnam and Afghanistan, besides the fact that there was water in one of the places and not in the other was in Vietnam, they didn't have explosives for their improvised devices. They didn't have leftover artillery shells. So what they would do instead of an artillery shell on a cell phone detonator, the Viet Cong would dig a hole and put a camouflage on top of it and gets sharp sticks, literally sharp pieces of wood, called punji sticks. They would put the sticks in the bottom of the hole so when someone stepped in the hole, their foot and lower leg would get pierced by the sticks. The Viet Cong also wanted to make sure, or as sure as they could, that whoever stepped on one of these sticks would not only have the punji go through and cause all sorts of damage, but they wanted it the wound to get infected if at all possible. So they smeared the sticks with poop because they wanted the infection too.

A lot of folks treat mistakes kind of like stepping on a punji stick. Once they make the mistake, they start allowing it to poison things, "Oh, that mistake, oh, I wish I hadn't done that." "I so messed things up..." It poisons everything. It poisons their thinking. It poisons the relationship with people who were present when the mistake happened. It poisons their ability to go back where the mistake happened. It poisons everything...

That's not helpful – but it's often what happens if they're not denying it entirely.

A better way, and lots and lots of gurus out there will teach you this, when you make a mistake, you forget it, and drive on. Right? Who's heard this before? Forget it, drive on. You treat it like a pothole, at least in American pothole. I've seen pictures of potholes in other countries that'll swallow the car. But here the worse a pothole will do, is kind of knock you off course a little bit and you just pull the wheel and you get back on course. You forget it and drive on, and it's not a bad idea. It's much better than letting it poison you.

Just forget it and drive on – but it's not the genius way to treat mistakes...

Who recognizes this guy? Thomas Edison. What has he got there? A light bulb. How many mistakes did he make when he was building the light bulb?

Zero...

Because every single time he made a filament and it failed, and I heard about a thousand times, every single time it failed – that mistake was a portal of discovery. A learning experience.

It's not, "I'm going to focus on this and let it poison everything because I'm only looking at the problem – the mistake I made."

It's not, "Forget it drive on."

It's, "All right – that didn't work. Why didn't it work? What can I learn from it? What can I do to make the next time more likely to succeed?" And then you step through that portal of discovery toward a brighter future.

The difference is between the stimulus of making a mistake and the response is that space. Which choice do I make?

Is it going to be a punji...

Or a pothole...

Or a portal?

www.ingramcontent.com/pod-product-compliance
Lightning Source LLC
Chambersburg PA
CBHW030543220526
45463CB00007B/2964

A thoroughly enjoyable read, this book has many of the management tools you would normally see in a full day management seminar in Cliffs Notes format. Written in clear, concise terms it is a good read.
The examples used to explain the management ideas are quite well chosen and easy to adapt to any area of business.
Well worth the time to read and one of those books that should be kept in the top desk drawer for later review.

— Richard Haynes